Flower Basket Panel Filet Crochet Pattern

Flower Basket Panel Filet Crochet Pattern

Complete Instructions and Chart

designed by Emma Loper

edited by Claudia Botterweg

EIGHTTHREEPRESS
Phoenix, Arizona, USA

Original pattern design by Emma Loper, first published in 1921
Pattern rewritten, expanded, edited and charted by Claudia Botterweg,
published in 2017 by Eight Three Press
ISBN-13: 978-1979824316
ISBN-10: 1979824312
Every effort has been made to ensure that all the infor-
mation in this book is accurate. If you have questions or
comments about this pattern, please contact Claudia Botterweg at
http://claudiabotterweg.com/contact

Contents

Introduction

In many homes will be found one or more of the old-time "tidies"—veritable heirlooms—wrought by hands perhaps long since folded in peaceful rest, and so all the more precious. Most of these are done in "block-and-space work", renamed in later years "filet crochet", because of its resemblance to the real filet-darned netting, or Gitteryl embroidery. Whatever the name, however, the work surely does not suffer in comparison with that of the present time, so firm and even it is, and the designs as a rule are naturalistic and graceful.

The flower basket pattern appears in many phases, and a particularly attractive variation is presented, very pleasing for pillow-top or windowpane.

Size & Yardage

The approximate size of the finished piece will change when made with different sizes of thread and hooks. Approximate yardage needed for each thread size varies also.

For best results, make a gauge swatch before you begin.

Size 5 thread (about 3.6 squares/inch)
Width: 29 ⅔", Height: 40"
Amount of thread required: 2,400 yards
Suggested hook: Size 3 steel

Size 10 thread (about 4.3 squares/inch)
Width: 24 ⅓", Height: 31 ¼"
Amount of thread required: 1,525 yards
Suggested hook: Size 7 steel

Size 20 thread (about 4.5 squares/inch)
Width: 23 ⅓", Height: 30"
Amount of thread required: 1,425 yards
Suggested hook: Size 10 steel

Size 30 thread (about 4.7 squares/inch)
Width: 22 ¼", Height: 28 ¾"
Amount of thread required: 1,330 yards
Suggested hook: Size 11 steel

Size 50 thread (about 6 squares/inch)
   Width: 17", Height: 22 ½"
   Amount of thread required: 760 yards
   Suggested hook: Size 12 steel

Size 80 thread (about 7 squares/inch)
   Width: 15", Height: 20"
   Amount of thread required: 600 yards
   Suggested hook: Size 14 steel

Flower Basket Written Instructions

Abbreviations used in this pattern
    ( ) work instructions within parentheses as many times as directed
    * * work instructions within asterisks as many times as directed
    ch: chain stitch
    dc: double crochet
    sk: skip the indicated amount of stitches
    sl st: slip stitch
    space: ch 2, sk 2, dc in next stitch. For first space in a row, ch 5, sk 2, dc in next stitch.
    block: 3 dc. For first block in a row, ch 3 for outside "post", then 3 dc as usual.

Chain 323.
    Row 1: Dc in 8th stitch from hook, 105 more spaces, turn. 106 squares.
    If you wish, make 1st row of spaces thus, omitting the long foundation chain: Chain 8, dc in 1st stitch of chain, * turn, chain 5, dc in 3rd stitch of preceding chain; repeat until you have the requisite number of squares.
    Rows 2 – 10: 106 spaces, turn.
    Row 11: 30 spaces, 2 blocks, 18 spaces, 3 blocks, 53 spaces, turn.
    Row 12: 49 spaces, 2 blocks, 2 spaces, 3 blocks, 2 spaces, 2 blocks, 10 spaces, 2 blocks, 2 spaces, 3 blocks, 2 spaces, 2 blocks, 25 spaces, turn.
    Row 13: 25 spaces, 3 blocks, (1 space, 3 blocks) twice, 10 spaces, (3 blocks, 1 space) twice, 3 blocks, 12 spaces, 1 block, 36 spaces, turn.

Row 14: 35 spaces, 3 blocks, 8 spaces, 2 blocks, 2 spaces, 3 blocks, 1 space, 1 block, 1 space, 3 blocks, 5 spaces, 1 block, 6 spaces, 3 blocks, 1 space, 1 block, 1 space, 3 blocks, 26 spaces, turn.

Row 15: 29 spaces, 1 block, 1 space, 1 block, 9 spaces, 3 blocks, 6 spaces, 1 block, 1 space, 1 block, 4 spaces, 3 blocks, 9 spaces, 1 block, 36 spaces, turn.

Row 16: 37 spaces, 1 block, 9 spaces, 2 blocks, 4 spaces, 3 blocks, 1 space, 2 blocks, 2 spaces, 4 blocks, 9 spaces, 3 blocks, 29 spaces, turn.

Row 17: 27 spaces, 1 block, 1 space, 3 blocks, 10 spaces, 3 blocks, 1 space, 2 blocks, 2 spaces, 3 blocks, 4 spaces, 1 block, 8 spaces, 1 block, 1 space, 1 block, 37 spaces, turn.

Row 18: 18 spaces, 3 blocks, 16 spaces, 4 blocks, 4 spaces, 3 blocks, 1 space, 3 blocks, 3 spaces, 1 block, 2 spaces, 2 blocks, 1 space, 1 block, 5 spaces, 2 blocks, 6 spaces, 1 block, 1 space, 1 block, 28 spaces, turn.

Row 19: 29 spaces, 1 block, 7 spaces, 2 blocks, 2 spaces, 1 block, 3 spaces, 2 blocks, 2 spaces, 1 block, 2 spaces, 4 blocks, 1 space, 4 blocks, 5 spaces, 1 block, 2 spaces, 1 block, 1 space, 1 block, 14 spaces, 1 block, 19 spaces, turn.

Row 20: 19 spaces, 1 block, 1 space, 1 block, 12 spaces, 1 block, 1 space, 1 block, 8 spaces, 3 blocks, 1 space, (3 blocks, 2 spaces) twice, 1 block, 4 spaces, 2 blocks, 1 space, 1 block, 8 spaces, 1 block, 1 space, 2 blocks, 26 spaces, turn.

Row 21: 26 spaces, 2 blocks, 1 space, 1 block, 2 spaces, 2 blocks, 5 spaces, 3 blocks, 5 spaces, 2 blocks, 2 spaces, 1 block, 5 spaces, 1 block, 12 spaces, 1 block, 5 spaces, 1 block, 6 spaces, 4 blocks, 19 spaces, turn.

Row 22: 16 spaces, 1 block, 2 spaces, 1 block, 1 space, 1 block, 6 spaces, 3 blocks, 3 spaces, 1 block, 1 space, 1 block, 10 spaces, 2 blocks, 2 spaces, 3 blocks, 5 spaces, 2 blocks, 5 spaces, 1 block, 5 spaces, 3 blocks, 1 space, 2 blocks, 28 spaces, turn.

Row 23: 29 spaces, 1 block, 1 space, 2 blocks, 7 spaces, 5 blocks, 2 spaces, 2 blocks, 3 spaces, 4 blocks, 1 space, 3 blocks, 12 spaces,

3 blocks, 1 space, 1 block, 9 spaces, 1 block, 1 space, 3 blocks, 15 spaces, turn.

Row 24: 16 spaces, 1 block, 1 space, 2 blocks, 2 spaces, 1 block, 6 spaces, 2 blocks, 15 spaces, 2 blocks, 2 spaces, 2 blocks, 14 spaces, 2 blocks, 7 spaces, 1 block, 30 spaces, turn.

Row 25: 30 spaces, 1 block, 6 spaces, 1 block, 2 spaces, 2 blocks, 35 spaces, 1 block, 5 spaces, 1 block, 1 space, 1 block, 20 spaces, turn.

Row 26: 21 spaces, 1 block, 3 spaces, 1 block, 1 space, 1 block, 5 spaces, 1 block, 12 spaces, 13 blocks, 5 spaces, 1 block, (4 spaces, 1 block) twice, 31 spaces, turn.

Row 27: 32 spaces, 1 block, 3 spaces, 1 block, 7 spaces, 19 blocks, 8 spaces, 3 blocks, 5 spaces, 1 block, 3 spaces, 1 block, 1 space, 1 block, 20 spaces, turn.

Row 28: 19 spaces, 3 blocks, (1 space, 1 block) twice, 7 spaces, 1 block, 2 spaces, 1 block, 5 spaces, 5 blocks, 11 spaces, 5 blocks, 7 spaces, 1 block, 2 spaces, 1 block, 32 spaces, turn.

Row 29: 33 spaces, 1 block, 1 space, 1 block, 7 spaces, 3 blocks, 3 spaces, 3 blocks, 1 space, 1 block, 1 space, 3 blocks, 3 spaces, 3 blocks, 4 spaces, 4 blocks, 8 spaces, 1 block, 1 space, 1 block, 2 spaces, 1 block, 20 spaces, turn.

Row 30: 24 spaces, 1 block, 1 space, 2 blocks, 6 spaces, 1 block, 1 space, 1 block, 5 spaces, 3 blocks, 1 space, (1 block, 5 spaces) twice, 1 block, 1 space, 3 blocks, 4 spaces, 2 blocks, 2 spaces, 1 block, 34 spaces, turn.

Row 31: 24 spaces, 2 blocks, 1 space, 2 blocks, 5 spaces, 1 block, 1 space, 2 blocks, 4 spaces, 2 blocks, 6 spaces, 1 block, 5 spaces, 1 block, 6 spaces, 2 blocks, 7 spaces, 1 block, 6 spaces, 1 block, 1 space, 1 block, 24 spaces, turn.

Row 32: 23 spaces, 2 blocks, 6 spaces, 1 block, 1 space, 1 block, 7 spaces, 1 block, (1 space, 2 blocks) twice, 1 space, 1 block, 1 space, 3 blocks, 1 space, 1 block, (1 space, 2 blocks) twice, 1 space, 1 block, 5 spaces, 3 blocks, 4 spaces, 2 blocks, 1 space, 4 blocks, 23 spaces, turn.

Row 33: 24 spaces, 2 blocks, 1 space, 3 blocks, 3 spaces, 1 block, 8 spaces, 1 block, 7 spaces, 1 block, 5 spaces, 1 block, 7 spaces, 1 block, 3 spaces, 1 block, 1 space, 2 blocks, 1 space, 1 block, (3 spaces, 1 block) twice, 24 spaces, turn.

Row 34: 22 spaces, 1 block, 1 space, 1 block, (4 spaces, 3 blocks) twice, (1 space, 2 blocks) twice, 1 space, (1 block, 5 spaces) twice, (1 space, 2 blocks) twice, 7 spaces, 1 block, 2 spaces, 1 block, 30 spaces, turn.

Row 35: 17 spaces, 1 block, 1 space, 1 block, 11 spaces, 1 block, 1 space, 3 blocks, (5 spaces, 1 block) twice, (1 space, 3 blocks, 1 space, 1 block) twice, 5 spaces, 1 block, 2 spaces, 1 block, 4 spaces, (1 block, 3 spaces) twice, 4 blocks, 21 spaces, turn.

Row 36: 22 spaces, 1 block, 2 spaces, 1 block, 1 space, 1 block, 3 spaces, 3 blocks, 5 spaces, 2 blocks, 2 spaces, 2 blocks, 7 spaces, 1 block, 7 spaces, 2 blocks, 2 spaces, 2 blocks, 7 spaces, 1 block, 13 spaces, 1 block, 18 spaces, turn.

Row 37: 16 spaces, 3 blocks, 9 spaces, 3 blocks, 1 space, 1 block, 7 spaces, 1 block, 1 space, 1 block, 21 spaces, 1 block, 1 space, 1 block, 6 spaces, 1 block, 4 spaces, 1 block, 1 space, 1 block, 25 spaces, turn.

Row 38: 25 spaces, 1 block, 1 space, 1 block, 10 spaces, 2 blocks, 4 spaces, 17 blocks, 4 spaces, 2 blocks, 4 spaces, 1 block, (1 space, 2 blocks) twice, 9 spaces, 3 blocks, 16 spaces, turn.

Row 39: 17 spaces, 1 block, 14 spaces, 1 block, 1 space, 1 block, 4 spaces, 2 blocks, 1 space, 23 blocks, 1 space, 2 blocks, 11 spaces, 1 block, 12 spaces, 2 blocks, 12 spaces, turn.

Row 40: 12 spaces, 4 blocks, 10 spaces, 1 block, 10 spaces, 8 blocks, 15 spaces, 8 blocks, 4 spaces, 1 block, 15 spaces, 1 block, 1 space, 2 blocks, 14 spaces, turn.

Row 41: 14 spaces, 2 blocks, 1 space, 1 block, 14 spaces, 2 blocks, 4 spaces, 4 blocks, (5 spaces, 1 block) 3 times, 5 spaces, 4 blocks, 6 spaces, 1 block, 2 spaces, 1 block, 1 space, 2 blocks, 7 spaces, 5 blocks, 12 spaces, turn.

Row 42: 12 spaces, 6 blocks, 4 spaces, 4 blocks, (1 space, 1 block) twice, 6 spaces, 2 blocks, 4 spaces, (3 blocks, 1 space, 1 block, 1 space) 3 times, 3 blocks, 4 spaces, 2 blocks, 3 spaces, 1 block, 16 spaces, 2 blocks, 15 spaces, turn.

Row 43: 16 spaces, 1 block, 2 spaces, 1 block, 1 space, 1 block, 8 spaces, 2 blocks, (2 spaces, 1 block) twice, 3 spaces, 1 block, 11 spaces, 1 block, 5 spaces, 1 block, 4 spaces, 2 blocks, (1 space, 1 block) twice, 6 spaces, (1 block, 1 space) twice, 4 blocks, 3 spaces, 6 blocks, 13 spaces, turn.

Row 44: 13 spaces, 2 blocks, 1 space, (4 blocks, 2 spaces) twice, 1 block, 6 spaces, 2 blocks, 6 spaces, (1 block, 5 spaces) twice, (1 block, 2 spaces) twice, 1 block, 4 spaces, 1 block, 1 space, 2 blocks, 1 space, 1 block, 1 space, 4 blocks, 8 spaces, 3 blocks, 1 space, 1 block, 1 space, 2 blocks, 13 spaces, turn.

Row 45: 14 spaces, (1 block, 1 space) twice, 2 blocks, 10 spaces, 1 block, 2 spaces, 2 blocks, 1 space, 1 block, 2 spaces, 1 block, 1 space, 2 blocks, 1 space, 1 block, 1 space, 5 blocks, (1 space, 3 blocks, 1 space, 1 block) twice, (1 space, 2 blocks) twice, 1 space, 1 block, 6 spaces, 1 block, 2 spaces, 2 blocks, 1 space, 2 blocks, (1 space, 3 blocks) twice, 13 spaces, turn.

Row 46: 13 spaces, 4 blocks, (1 space, 2 blocks) 3 times, 3 spaces, 1 block, 4 spaces, 2 blocks, 7 spaces, 1 block, 5 spaces, 1 block, 7 spaces, 3 blocks, 1 space, 1 block, 6 spaces, 3 blocks, 2 spaces, 1 block, 13 spaces, 1 block, 1 space, 2 blocks, 15 spaces, turn.

Row 47: 16 spaces, 1 block, 1 space, 1 block, 2 spaces, 1 block, 1 space, 1 block, 11 spaces, 1 block, 3 spaces, 1 block, 6 spaces, 3 blocks, 1 space, 4 blocks, (5 spaces, 1 block) twice, 1 space, 2 blocks, (2 spaces, 1 block) twice, 1 space, 1 block, 3 spaces, (2 blocks, 1 space) twice, 6 blocks, 14 spaces, turn.

Row 48: 15 spaces, 5 blocks, 1 space, 1 block, 1 space, 2 blocks, 3 spaces, 1 block, 1 space, 1 block, 2 spaces, 2 blocks, 2 spaces, 1 block, 2 spaces, (1 block, 1 space, 3 blocks, 1 space) twice, 8 blocks, 2 spaces, 3 blocks, (1 space, 1 block) twice, 1 space, 2 blocks, 11 spaces, 3 blocks, (1 space, 1 block) twice, 16 spaces, turn.

Row 49: 15 spaces, 1 block, 1 space, 1 block, 3 spaces, 2 blocks, 11 spaces, 1 block, 6 spaces, 4 blocks, 1 space, 2 blocks, 1 space, 5 blocks, (5 spaces, 1 block) twice, 4 spaces, 1 block, (1 space, 1 block) twice, 7 spaces, 3 blocks, 1 space, 2 blocks, 18 spaces, turn.

Row 50: 20 spaces, 1 block, 1 space, 1 block, 2 spaces, 2 blocks, 5 spaces, 2 blocks, 3 spaces, 2 blocks, 4 spaces, 1 block, 5 spaces, (1 block, 1 space) twice, 4 blocks, 1 space, 7 blocks, 1 space, 2 blocks, 1 space, 1 block, 1 space, 2 blocks, 10 spaces, 2 blocks, 3 spaces, 2 blocks, 16 spaces, turn.

Row 51: 18 spaces, 1 block, 2 spaces, 1 block, 3 spaces, 1 block, 6 spaces, 2 blocks, 8 spaces, 4 blocks, 1 space, 1 block, 1 space, 3 blocks, 4 spaces, 1 block, 1 space, 3 blocks, (1 space, 1 block) twice, 6 spaces, 1 block, 1 space, 2 blocks, 3 spaces, 3 blocks, 3 spaces, 6 blocks, 16 spaces, turn.

Row 52: 13 spaces, 6 blocks, (1 space, 1 block) twice, 3 spaces, (2 blocks, 2 spaces) twice, 1 block, (1 space, 2 blocks) twice, 2 spaces, 1 block, 8 spaces, 2 blocks, 2 spaces, 5 blocks, 4 spaces, 2 blocks, 2 spaces, 1 block, 3 spaces, 2 blocks, 4 spaces, 2 blocks, 3 spaces, 1 block, 1 space, 1 block, 19 spaces, turn.

Row 53: 18 spaces, 1 block, 1 space, 2 blocks, 1 space, 1 block, 1 space, 2 blocks, 3 spaces, 2 blocks, 2 spaces, 1 block, 7 spaces, 3 blocks, 2 spaces, 1 block, 2 spaces, 4 blocks, 1 space, 3 blocks, 14 spaces, 1 block, 2 spaces, 2 blocks, 2 spaces, 1 block, 1 space, (2 blocks, 2 spaces) twice, 6 blocks, 11 spaces, turn.

Row 54: 12 spaces, 9 blocks, 4 spaces, 2 blocks, 1 space, 2 blocks, 5 spaces, 16 blocks, 1 space, 4 blocks, 1 space, 1 block, 2 spaces, 4 blocks, 1 space, 5 blocks, 5 spaces, 2 blocks, 3 spaces, 1 block, 1 space, 2 blocks, 22 spaces, turn.

Row 55: 21 spaces, 1 block, 2 spaces, 2 blocks, 2 spaces, 13 blocks, 1 space, 5 blocks, 1 space, 1 block, 1 space, 3 blocks, 1 space, 25 blocks, 2 spaces, 3 blocks, 2 spaces, 6 blocks, 14 spaces, turn.

Row 56: 22 spaces, 2 blocks, 2 spaces, 22 blocks, 8 spaces, 1 block, 1 space, 6 blocks, 1 space, 15 blocks, 26 spaces, turn.

Row 57: 25 spaces, 10 blocks, 9 spaces, 4 blocks, 2 spaces, 3 blocks, 1 space, 2 blocks, 6 spaces, 2 blocks, 8 spaces, 9 blocks, 25 spaces, turn.

Row 58: 24 spaces, 4 blocks, 6 spaces, 7 blocks, 1 space, 2 blocks, 1 space, 1 block, 1 space, 3 blocks, 2 spaces, 5 blocks, 7 spaces, 5 blocks, 5 spaces, 8 blocks, 24 spaces, turn.

Row 59: 24 spaces, 5 blocks, 3 spaces, 3 blocks, 3 spaces, 4 blocks, 2 spaces, 4 blocks, (1 space, 5 blocks) twice, 2 spaces, 2 blocks, 1 space, 2 blocks, (2 spaces, 3 blocks) twice, 2 spaces, 4 blocks, 23 spaces, turn.

Row 60: 23 spaces, 3 blocks, 2 spaces, 5 blocks, 2 spaces, 4 blocks, 3 spaces, 2 blocks, 1 space, 9 blocks, 1 space, 3 blocks, 1 space, 4 blocks, (1 space, 3 blocks) twice, 1 space, 1 block, 1 space, 3 blocks, 2 spaces, 3 blocks, 24 spaces, turn.

Row 61: 25 spaces, 3 blocks, 1 space, 4 blocks, (1 space, 5 blocks) twice, 4 spaces, 2 blocks, 1 space, 5 blocks, 1 space, 3 blocks, 1 space, 2 blocks, 1 space, 5 blocks, 2 spaces, 4 blocks, 3 spaces, 4 blocks, 23 spaces, turn.

Row 62: 19 spaces, 1 block, 4 spaces, 7 blocks, 3 spaces, 2 blocks, 6 spaces, 2 blocks, 1 space, 4 blocks, 2 spaces, 5 blocks, 1 space, 4 blocks, 2 spaces, 1 block, 1 space, 5 blocks, 2 spaces, 1 block, 3 spaces, 2 blocks, 1 space, 10 blocks, 26 spaces, turn.

Row 63: 15 spaces, 1 block, 8 spaces, 1 block, 3 spaces, 3 blocks, 1 space, 4 blocks, 1 space, 2 blocks, 2 spaces, 1 block, 2 spaces, 7 blocks, 2 spaces, 2 blocks, (1 space, 3 blocks) twice, 1 space, 8 blocks, 4 spaces, 2 blocks, 19 spaces, turn.

Row 64: 19 spaces, 3 blocks, 2 spaces, 1 block, 5 spaces, (5 blocks, 1 space) twice, 4 blocks, 3 spaces, 3 blocks, 1 space, 2 blocks, 1 space, 1 block, 3 spaces, 2 blocks, 2 spaces, 1 block, 2 spaces, 2 blocks, 1 space, 3 blocks, 1 space, 2 blocks, 4 spaces, 1 block, 8 spaces, 2 blocks, 15 spaces, turn.

Row 65: 15 spaces, 3 blocks, 6 spaces, 1 block, (1 space, 3 blocks) twice, (1 space, 4 blocks) twice, 1 space, 6 blocks, 1 space, 1 block, 2 spaces, 5 blocks, 1 space, 1 block, (1 space, 2 blocks) twice, 1 space, 6 blocks, 1 space, 3 blocks, 2 spaces, 2 blocks, 1 space, 4 blocks, 19 spaces, turn.

Row 66: 20 spaces, 4 blocks, 1 space, 1 block, 2 spaces, 4 blocks, 4 spaces, 1 block, 1 space, (2 blocks, 2 spaces) twice, 4 blocks, 2 spaces, 1 block, (1 space, 7 blocks) twice, 2 spaces, 6 blocks, 2 spaces, 1 block, 4 spaces, 1 block, 3 spaces, 4 blocks, 14 spaces, turn.

Row 67: 14 spaces, 2 blocks, 1 space, 2 blocks, 2 spaces, 2 blocks, 5 spaces, 6 blocks, 1 space, 2 blocks, 1 space, 1 block, 3 spaces, 2 blocks, 2 spaces, 10 blocks, 1 space, 3 blocks, 2 spaces, 2 blocks, (1 space, 4 blocks) twice, (1 space, 2 blocks) twice, 2 spaces, 2 blocks, 22 spaces, turn.

Row 68: 19 spaces, 2 blocks, 3 spaces, 2 blocks, 2 spaces, 2 blocks, 1 space, 6 blocks, 1 space, 1 block, 1 space, 4 blocks, 2 spaces, 7 blocks, (1 space, 3 blocks) twice, 1 space, 6 blocks, 1 space, 1 block, 2 spaces, 1 block, 3 spaces, 2 blocks, 4 spaces, 3 blocks, 2 spaces, 2 blocks, 1 space, 2 blocks, 14 spaces, turn.

Row 69: 14 spaces, (2 blocks, 1 space) twice, 4 blocks, 2 spaces, 1 block, 1 space, 7 blocks, 2 spaces, 6 blocks, 1 space, 3 blocks, 1 space, 4 blocks, 1 space, 6 blocks, 3 spaces, 6 blocks, 1 space, 2 blocks, 2 spaces, 2 blocks, 1 space, 2 blocks, 4 spaces, 2 blocks, 1 space, 4 blocks, 17 spaces, turn.

Row 70: 17 spaces, 7 blocks, 5 spaces, (1 block, 1 space) 3 times, 2 blocks, 1 space, 2 blocks, 2 spaces, 5 blocks, 4 spaces, 2 blocks, 1 space, 8 blocks, 3 spaces, 3 blocks, 1 space, 2 blocks, 1 space, 5 blocks, 2 spaces, 2 blocks, (1 space, 4 blocks) twice, 15 spaces, turn.

Row 71: 16 spaces, 3 blocks, 1 space, 4 blocks, 1 space, 3 blocks, 3 spaces, 3 blocks, 1 space, 7 blocks, 2 spaces, (5 blocks, 1 space) twice, (2 blocks, 1 space) 4 times, 1 block, 1 space, 2 blocks, 1 space, 1 block, 2 spaces, (1 block, 1 space) twice, 11 blocks, 15 spaces, turn.

Row 72: 14 spaces, 4 blocks, 4 spaces, 4 blocks, 1 space, 1 block, 3 spaces, 1 block, 1 space, 2 blocks, 1 space, 5 blocks, 1 space, 2 blocks, 3 spaces, 3 blocks, 2 spaces, 3 blocks, 3 spaces, (4 blocks, 1 space)

3 times, 2 blocks, 3 spaces, 3 blocks, 2 spaces, 3 blocks, 1 space, 2 blocks, 17 spaces, turn.

Row 73: 14 spaces, 3 blocks, 2 spaces, 1 block, 1 space, 2 blocks, 2 spaces, 1 block, 1 space, 1 block, 3 spaces, 5 blocks, 1 space, 2 blocks, 1 space, 3 blocks, 1 space, 1 block, 3 spaces, 3 blocks, 3 spaces, 2 blocks, 1 space, 3 blocks, 2 spaces, (2 blocks, 1 space) twice, 3 blocks, 2 spaces, (1 block, 1 space) twice, 1 block, 2 spaces, (3 blocks, 1 space) twice, 4 blocks, 14 spaces, turn.

Row 74: 14 spaces, 4 blocks, 1 space, 3 blocks, 1 space, 2 blocks, 1 space, 1 block, 2 spaces, (1 block, 1 space) twice, 5 blocks, 4 spaces, 2 blocks, 2 spaces, 2 blocks, 1 space, 3 blocks, 1 space, 2 blocks, 1 space, 3 blocks, 2 spaces, 1 block, 1 space, 6 blocks, 1 space, 5 blocks, 3 spaces, 1 block, 1 space, 1 block, 3 spaces, 2 blocks, 1 space, 6 blocks, 13 spac;es, turn.

Row 75: 21 spaces, 1 block, 4 spaces, 1 block, 5 spaces, 3 blocks, 2 spaces, 5 blocks, 2 spaces, 1 block, (1 space, 3 blocks) 3 times, 1 space, (2 blocks, 2 spaces) twice, 1 block, 2 spaces, 2 blocks, 4 spaces, 1 block, 1 space, 3 blocks, 2 spaces, 1 block, 1 space, 3 blocks, 2 spaces, 2 blocks, 15 spaces, turn.

Row 76: 18 spaces, 2 blocks, 2 spaces, 4 blocks, 4 spaces, 1 block, 6 spaces, 3 blocks, 2 spaces, 2 blocks, 1 space, 6 blocks, 1 space, 2 blocks, 1 space, 1 block, 1 space, 3 blocks, 1 space, 1 block, 3 spaces, 3 blocks, 1 space, 2 blocks, 3 spaces, 1 block, 4 spaces, 1 block, 2 spaces, 2 blocks, 1 space, 4 blocks, 17 spaces, turn.

Row 77: 15 spaces, 4 blocks, 1 space, 1 block, (3 spaces, 2 blocks) twice, 1 space, 1 block, 1 space, 3 blocks, 4 spaces, 1 block, 2 spaces, 1 block, 5 spaces, 4 blocks, 2 spaces, 4 blocks 1 space, 3 blocks, 2 spaces, 3 blocks, 4 spaces, 1 block, 2 spaces, 1 block, 3 spaces, 5 blocks, 2 spaces, 2 blocks, 17 spaces, turn.

Row 78: 17 spaces, 2 blocks, 2 spaces, 5 blocks, 3 spaces, (2 blocks, 2 spaces) twice, 3 blocks, 2 spaces, 2 blocks, 1 space, 1 block, 1 space, 3 blocks, 2 spaces, 4 blocks, 5 spaces, 1 block, 2 spaces, 1 block, 1 space, 1 block, 7 spaces, 1 block, 2 spaces, 3 blocks, 5 spaces, 2 blocks, 2 spaces, 3 blocks, 14 spaces, turn.

Row 79: 14 spaces, 6 blocks, 3 spaces, 4 blocks, 4 spaces, 1 block, 2 spaces, 3 blocks, 3 spaces, (1 block, 1 space) twice, 1 block, 5 spaces, 4 blocks, 4 spaces, (1 block, 1 space) twice, 3 blocks, (2 spaces, 2 blocks) twice, 9 spaces, 3 blocks, 2 spaces, 1 block, 1 space, 2 blocks, 15 spaces, turn.

Row 80: 17 spaces, 2 blocks, 14 spaces, 3 blocks, 2 spaces, (1 block, 1 space) twice, 2 blocks, 1 space, 1 block, 7 spaces, 2 blocks, 5 spaces, 2 blocks, 3 spaces, 1 block, 2 spaces, 5 blocks, 2 spaces, 3 blocks, 1 space, 1 block, 1 space, 4 blocks, 2 spaces, 5 blocks, 14 spaces, turn.

Row 81: 20 spaces, 4 blocks, 1 space, 7 blocks, 1 space, 6 blocks, 5 spaces, 2 blocks, 5 spaces, 1 block, 8 spaces, 1 block, 1 space, 2 blocks, (2 spaces, 2 blocks) twice, 15 spaces, 1 block, 1 space, 1 block, 16 spaces, turn.

Row 82: 34 spaces, 2 blocks, 3 spaces, 1 block, 2 spaces, 3 blocks, 15 spaces, 2 blocks, 5 spaces, 3 blocks, 1 space, 2 blocks, 1 space; 5 blocks, 1 space, 2 blocks, 2 spaces, 2 blocks, 20 spaces, turn.

Row 83: 19 spaces, 7 blocks, 1 space, 2 blocks, (1 space, 4 blocks) twice, 4 spaces, 1 block, 1 space, 1 block, 15 spaces, 2 blocks, 2 spaces, 1 block, 1 space, 1 block, 2 spaces, 2 blocks, 4 spaces, 1 block, 29 spaces, turn.

Row 84: 30 spaces, 2 blocks, 3 spaces, 1 block, 1 space, (1 block, 2 spaces) twice, 2 blocks, 15 spaces, 1 block, 1 space, 1 block, 5 spaces, (3 blocks, 1 space) twice, 3 blocks, 2 spaces, 6 blocks, 19 spaces, turn.

Row 85: 19 spaces, 4 blocks, 2 spaces, (2 blocks, 1 space) 3 times, 3 blocks, 5 spaces, 1 block, 2 spaces, 2 blocks, 14 spaces, 3 blocks, 5 spaces, 1 block, 3 spaces, 3 blocks, 30 spaces, turn.

Row 86: 31 spaces, 2 blocks, 3 spaces, 1 block, 4 spaces, 1 block, 1 space, 2 blocks, 14 spaces, 2 blocks, 3 spaces, 2 blocks, 1 space, 6 blocks, 2 spaces, 7 blocks, 24 spaces, turn.

Row 87: 24 spaces, 2 blocks, 3 spaces, 1 block, 2 spaces, 1 block, 1 space, 6 blocks, 1 space, 1 block, 3 spaces, 2 blocks, 14 spaces, 2 blocks, 1 space, 2 blocks, 2 spaces, 1 block, (1 space, 2 blocks) twice, 31 spaces, turn.

Row 88: 26 spaces, 1 block, 4 spaces, 2 blocks, 2 spaces, 1 block, 1 space, 1 block, 3 spaces, 1 block, 1 space, 3 blocks, 12 spaces, 2 blocks, 3 spaces, 1 block, 2 spaces, 3 blocks, 2 spaces, 1 block, 1 space, 2 blocks, 1 space, 6 blocks, 24 spaces, turn.

Row 89: 25 spaces, 6 blocks, 2 spaces, 7 blocks, (1 space, 1 block) twice, 2 spaces, 2 blocks, 4 spaces, 3 blocks, 5 spaces, 2 blocks, 3 spaces, 1 block, 5 spaces, 1 block, 1 space, 1 block, 3 spaces, 2 blocks, 27 spaces, turn.

Row 90: 27 spaces, 2 blocks, 3 spaces, 1 block, 1 space, 1 block, 4 spaces, 1 block, 4 spaces, 3 blocks, 3 spaces, 2 blocks, 1 space, 2 blocks, 3 spaces, 2 blocks, 2 spaces, 3 blocks, 2 spaces, (4 blocks, 1 space) twice, 3 blocks, 26 spaces, turn.

Row 91: 25 spaces, (3 blocks, 1 space) twice, 2 blocks, 1 space, 1 block, 5 spaces, 2 blocks, 3 spaces, 2 blocks, 2 spaces, 1 block, 1 space, 3 blocks, 3 spaces, 2 blocks, 3 spaces, 5 blocks, 3 spaces, 1 block, 3 spaces, 3 blocks, 27 spaces, turn.

Row 92: 27 spaces, 3 blocks, 3 spaces, 1 block, 2 spaces, 7 blocks, 2 spaces, 2 blocks, 3 spaces, 1 block, (1 space, 3 blocks) twice, 9 spaces, 1 block, 2 spaces, 2 blocks, 1 space, 7 blocks, 25 spaces, turn.

Row 93: 25 spaces, 12 blocks, 11 spaces, 6 blocks, 1 space, 1 block, 2 spaces, 1 block, 3 spaces, 7 blocks, 2 spaces, 1 block, 1 space, 2 blocks, 1 space, 3 blocks, 27 spaces, turn.

Row 94: 27 spaces, 3 blocks, 2 spaces, 1 block, 6 spaces, (1 block, 1 space) twice, 1 block, 3 spaces, 4 blocks, 1 space, 5 blocks, 10 spaces, 2 blocks, 2 spaces, 5 blocks, 1 space, 4 blocks, 25 spaces, turn.

Row 95: 26 spaces, 2 blocks, 3 spaces, 3 blocks, 3 spaces, 1 block, 13 spaces, 7 blocks, 3 spaces, 3 blocks, 2 spaces, 1 block, 6 spaces, 1 block, 3 spaces, 1 block, 28 spaces, turn.

Row 96: 24 spaces, 1 block, 4 spaces, 1 block, 2 spaces, 1 block, 5 spaces, 2 blocks, 3 spaces, 1 block, 1 space, 2 blocks, 2 spaces, 10 blocks, 16 spaces, 1 block, 30 spaces, turn.

Row 97: 24 spaces, 3 blocks, 2 spaces, 1 block, 13 spaces, 5 blocks, (1 space, 3 blocks, 1 space, 2 blocks) twice, 3 spaces, 2 blocks, 5 spaces, (1 block, 1 space) twice, 1 block, 2 spaces, 2 blocks, 25 spaces, turn.

Row 98: 25 spaces, 2 blocks, 2 spaces, 1 block, 1 space, 1 block, 7 spaces, 1 block, 5 spaces, 4 blocks, 2 spaces, 2 blocks, 4 spaces, 2 blocks, 1 space, 1 block, 1 space, 2 blocks, 10 spaces, 2 blocks, 1 space, 4 blocks, 25 spaces, turn.

Row 99: 28 spaces, 1 block, 2 spaces, 1 block, 9 spaces, 6 blocks, 5 spaces, 3 blocks, 11 spaces, 2 blocks, 6 spaces, (1 block, 1 space) twice, 3 blocks, 25 spaces, turn.

Row 100: 26 spaces, 2 blocks, 2 spaces, 1 block, 1 space, 1 block, 6 spaces, 1 block, 12 spaces, 3 blocks, 7 spaces, 1 block, 1 space, 1 block, 11 spaces, 1 block, 1 space, 3 blocks, 25 spaces, turn.

Row 101: 23 spaces, 3 blocks, (1 space, 1 block) twice, 4 spaces, 2 blocks, 1 space, 2 blocks, 27 spaces, 1 block, 6 spaces, 1 block, 1 space, 1 block, 2 spaces, 1 block, 27 spaces, turn.

Row 102: 28 spaces, 1 block, 1 space, 1 block, 7 spaces, 1 block, 1 space, 2 blocks, 23 spaces, 4 blocks, 1 space, 3 blocks, (2 spaces, 1 block) twice, 1 space, 4 blocks, 22 spaces, turn.

Row 103: 18 spaces, 1 block, 7 spaces, 1 block, 3 spaces, 1 block, 2 spaces, 3 blocks, 1 space, 4 blocks, 24 spaces, 1 block, 9 spaces, 2 blocks, 29 spaces, turn.

Row 104: 25 spaces, 1 block, 4 spaces, 1 block, 9 spaces, 1 block, 25 spaces, 3 blocks, 2 spaces, 2 blocks, 2 spaces, 1 block, 3 spaces, 1 block, 5 spaces, 2 blocks, 19 spaces, turn.

Row 105: 19 spaces, 3 blocks, 3 spaces, 1 block, 5 spaces, 1 block, 3 spaces, 2 blocks, 28 spaces, 2 blocks, 8 spaces, 1 block, 2 spaces, 2 blocks, 26 spaces, turn.

Row 106: 26 spaces, 3 blocks, 2 spaces, 2 blocks, 8 spaces, 2 blocks, 22 spaces, 3 blocks, 1 space, 2 blocks, 3 spaces, 1 block, 4 spaces, 1 block, 1 space, 3 blocks, 22 spaces, turn.

Row 107: 21 spaces, 1 block, 8 spaces, 1 block, 1 space, 3 blocks, 2 spaces, 4 blocks, 23 spaces, 1 block, 9 spaces, 5 blocks, 27 spaces, turn.

Row 108: 31 spaces, 1 block, 10 spaces, 1 block, 23 spaces, 2 blocks, 2 spaces, 1 block, 4 spaces, 2 blocks, 8 spaces, 1 block, 2 spaces, 3 blocks, 15 spaces, turn.

Row 109: 15 spaces, 4 blocks, 1 space, 1 block, 8 spaces, 2 blocks, 4 spaces, 1 block, 36 spaces, 2 blocks, 32 spaces, turn.

Row 110: 28 spaces, 3 blocks, 1 space, 1 block, 43 spaces, 1 block, 8 spaces, 2 blocks, 1 space, 3 blocks, 15 spaces, turn.

Row 111: 19 spaces, 2 blocks, 1 space, 2 blocks, 47 spaces, 2 blocks, 1 space, 3 blocks, 29 spaces, turn.

Row 112: 33 spaces, 1 block, 47 spaces, * 4 blocks, 1 space, 3 blocks, 17 spaces, turn.

Row 113: 17 spaces, 3 blocks, 1 space, 4 blocks, 42 spaces, 1 block, 3 spaces, 1 block, 1 space, 2 blocks, 31 spaces, turn.

Row 114: 35 spaces, 3 blocks, 45 spaces, 2 blocks, 1 space, 2 blocks, 18 spaces, turn.

Rows 115 – 125: 106 spaces, turn.

Finishing

Fringe may be knotted in at the edge, or a simple scallop may be added as a finish. One may use some pretty border in filet crochet, to serve as a sort of frame for the design, instead of the edge of plain spaces, if desired.

Flower Basket Chart

Chain 323, or see written instructions for an alternate way to make the first row.

Odd rows are worked left to right. Even rows are worked right to left.

Begin rows with ch 5 for the first space.

Hints & Tips

Use the best thread. Don't try to save a few pennies on the thread. You're not just making lace, you're making an heirloom!

Wash your hands before you pick up your project to work on. Keeping your hands clean while you work will help to avoid stains on your piece of lace.

When you're finished, weave in ends of thread by pulling the thread through several stitches with your hook.

To block your lace, dampen it and use a warm iron to block it in to shape. I like to use a little bit of spray starch to finish it off.

Filet crochet patterns are made up of two elements. The first is the space, which is made up of a double crochet, chain two, skip two stitches, and double crochet in the next stitch. The second is the block, which is made of a double crochet, double crochet in the next two stitches, and double crochet in the next stitch.

When you make a block over a space from the previous row, just double crochet into the space. Don't worry about crocheting into each chain.

You can follow a chart instead of a written pattern (a chart is included with this pattern). When you use the chart, you just need to remember that the beginning of each row starts with either chain three (for a block) or chain five (for a space). You can also use the chart to check your progress if you're using the written instructions.

Visit http://claudiabotterweg.com/crochet for tips, hints and more about lace crochet.

I hope you enjoyed making this beautiful piece of lace. Tell your friends where you got the pattern.

About the Editor

Claudia Botterweg learned how to crochet in third grade, and by the time she left home for college she had completed 8 rows on a ripple afghan. At Ohio State, she found herself living across the street from a vintage clothing store, and spent most of her budget on vintage clothes. She began repairing clothes in exchange for store credit. One of her tasks was to make camisoles with vintage crocheted lace yokes.

After college, Claudia inherited a tin full of several used balls of tatting thread, a tatting shuttle, and a size 14 steel crochet hook from her grandmother. She made some lace edgings from an old crochet pattern book, became fascinated with lace, and graduated to making doilies. In the 1980s, she made hundreds of lace collars and sold them at craft fairs. She also designed her own camisole yokes and made camisoles to sell.

Recently, Claudia acquired a stack of vintage patterns. She has been busily translating the patterns from vintage instructions, making them easy for beginning and intermediate crocheters to read. She is writing instructions when only charts were provided, and making charts when only written instructions were provided.

Claudia hopes that a new generation of crocheters will learn how to make beautiful lace to decorate themselves, their friends and families, and their homes.

http://ClaudiaBotterweg.com

More Patterns from Claudia Botterweg

Grape & Leaf Altar Lace Filet Crochet Pattern
Daffodil Altar Lace Filet Crochet Pattern
INRI Altar Lace Filet Crochet Pattern
Lily Altar Lace Filet Crochet Pattern
Quilt Block Lace Edging & Insertion Filet Crochet Pattern
Beverly Lace & Insertion Filet Crochet Pattern
Rose Lace & Insertion Filet Crochet Pattern
Morning Glory Lace & Insertion Filet Crochet Pattern
Rose Insertion Filet Crochet Pattern
Diamonds Insertion & Edging Filet Crochet Pattern
Rose and Butterfly Lace Border Filet Crochet Pattern
Clover Diamonds Edging & Insertion Filet Crochet Pattern
Marguerite Daisy Edging & Insertion Filet Crochet Pattern
Ivy Lace Scarf End Filet Crochet Pattern
Daffodil Lace Scarf End Filet Crochet Pattern
Rose Medallion Scarf End Filet Crochet Pattern
Lyre Lace Scarf End Filet Crochet Pattern
Grapes Lace Scarf End Filet Crochet Pattern
Bluebirds Scarf End Filet Crochet Pattern
Flower Pot Scarf End Filet Crochet Pattern
Dogwood Blossom Lace Curtain Filet Crochet Pattern
Two Peacocks Lace Curtain Filet Crochet Pattern
Two Dragons Lace Curtain Filet Crochet Pattern
Daffodil Lace Curtain Filet Crochet Pattern
Elegant Dragons Lace Curtain Filet Crochet Pattern
Regal Peacocks Lace Curtain Filet Crochet Pattern
Tropical Flowers Lace Curtain Filet Crochet Pattern
Garden Trellis Lace Centerpiece Filet Crochet Pattern

Clematis Lace Centerpiece Filet Crochet Pattern
Pennsylvania Dutch Tulips Tablecloth Filet Crochet Pattern
Fleur-de-lis Square Doily Filet Crochet Pattern
Nottingham Apple Lace Luncheon Set Filet Crochet Pattern
Chrysanthemum Lace 5-Piece Set Filet Crochet Pattern
Butterfly Lace Table Runner Filet Crochet Pattern
Daisy Lace Corners Filet Crochet Pattern
Carnation Lace Corners Filet Crochet Pattern
Butterfly Corners Luncheon Set Filet Crochet Pattern
Tulip Lace Panel Filet Crochet Pattern
Flower Basket with Butterfly Filet Crochet Pattern
Stork Wall Hanging Filet Crochet Pattern
Spirit of St. Louis Lace Panel Filet Crochet Pattern
Tall Ship Lace Filet Crochet Pattern
Lion Lace Panel Filet Crochet Pattern
Two Deer Lace Panel Filet Crochet Pattern
Folk Peacock Filet Crochet Pattern
Two Spring Lace Panels Filet Crochet Pattern
Snowflake Square Lace Pillow Cover Filet Crochet Pattern
Sailor Boy Lace Panel Filet Crochet Pattern
The Great Seal of the United States Filet Crochet Pattern
American Flag Lace Panel Filet Crochet Pattern
Veterans of Foreign Wars Panel Filet Crochet Pattern
26 Mix & Match Alphabet Insertions Filet Crochet Pattern
Seven Animal Insertions Filet Crochet Pattern
Animal Blocks Bedspread Filet Crochet Pattern
Medieval Tapestry Blocks Filet Crochet Pattern
Meandering Butterflies Bedspread Filet Crochet Pattern
Butterfly Lace Camisole Yoke Filet Crochet Pattern
Rose Bouquet Yoke with Sleeves Filet Crochet Pattern
Crochet Journal
Knitting Journal
Tatting Journal

Printed in Great Britain
by Amazon